On the Story

It's a big family!

by Brian Ogden

The Lord's Prayer for young readers

Acknowledgment

Mrs Gill Grainger, Head Teacher at Woolenwick First School in Stevenage, has made an invaluable contribution to this series by reading all the manuscripts and using the stories with her children.

Text copyright © 1999 Brian Ogden
Illustrations copyright © 1999 Simon Smith

The author asserts the moral right to be identified as the author of this work

Published by
The Bible Reading Fellowship
Peter's Way, Sandy Lane West
Oxford OX4 5HG
ISBN 1 84101 076 6

First edition 1999

10 9 8 7 6 5 4 3 2 1 0

All rights reserved

A catalogue record for this book is available from the British Library

Printed and bound in Great Britain by Caledonian International Book Manufacturing Ltd, Glasgow

Introduction

This is the sixth in a series of books for children starting school. The setting is a reception class. As with any classroom for younger children, the story mat is an important feature. Mrs Jolley, the reception teacher, often uses the story mat to tell the children Bible stories. In this book, the head teacher of Daisy Hill, Mrs Foster, introduces the Lord's Prayer. She relates the happenings in the school to the Lord's Prayer. It is hoped that teachers and parents will be able to choose stories which relate to their immediate circumstances and that the children will soon become friends with Mrs Jolley's children.

In this book there are seven stories, each dealing with one aspect of the Lord's Prayer. Prayers relating to each story are included for use in an assembly or with a story at bedtime. These are to be found at the end of the book.

So please come now and meet Mrs Foster, Mrs Jolley, together with David, Emma, James, Sarah, Joshua and his twin sister Rosie, Michael, Hannah and last, but not least, Sam. As it says on the classroom door...

Welcome to Mrs Jolley's Class

Contents

1. It's a big family! — 5
   Our Father, who art in heaven

2. Michael bumps his head — 14
   Thy will be done

3. I don't like cheese sandwiches any more — 21
   Give us this day our daily bread

4. 'I'm really sorry,' said Sarah — 29
   Forgive us our trespasses, as we forgive those who trespass against us

5. Mrs Foster finds a purse — 38
   Lead us not into temptation

6. Thunder and lightning — 46
   But deliver us from evil

7. The Hallelujah Chorus! — 54
   For thine is the kingdom, the power, and the glory, for ever and ever. Amen

Bible references and prayers — 62

It's a big family!

It was a big day for Mrs Jolley's class.

For the first time they were going into the whole school assembly.

The children lined up in the classroom.

David held Emma's hand.

James and Sarah walked together.

Joshua and Michael came next.

They were followed by Rosie and Hannah.

Mrs Jolley led the way down the long corridor.

They passed all the other classrooms.

As they got nearer the Big Hall, they heard music.

Mrs Jolley took them right up to the front of the Big Hall.

The children sat down.

In front of them was a table with a candle on it.

Standing by the table was Mrs Foster.

Mrs Foster was the head teacher.

She smiled at Mrs Jolley's class.

The other classes came into the Big Hall and sat down.

David whispered to Emma.

'I can see Tom over there.'

Tom was David's older brother.

Mrs Jolley looked at David.

She put her finger to her lips.

David knew that meant he shouldn't talk.

Mrs Foster stopped the music and lit the candle.

'Today,' she said, 'is a very special day.

It's the first time that Mrs Jolley's children have come to our assembly.

For the first time the whole school family is here.

Because all the family is here today, we will be thinking about the family prayer.

We call it the Lord's Prayer.

It's a prayer we often say in our assemblies.

One day,' said Mrs Foster, 'the friends of Jesus saw him praying.

Jesus was talking to God his Father.

When he finished praying, his friends went over to him.

"Jesus," they said, "please teach us how to pray."'

'Jesus,' said Mrs Foster, 'did a wonderful thing.

He taught them the words which we know now as the Lord's Prayer.

Sometimes we call it the Our Father prayer. Can anyone tell us why we call it the Our Father prayer?'

Lots of the older children put up their hands.

'Well, Amy?' asked Mrs Foster.

'Because it starts with Our Father,' said Amy.

'Well done,' said Mrs Foster.

'Jesus started his prayer by saying, "Our Father, who art in heaven, hallowed be thy name."

He wanted his friends to think about God as a loving father.

God is father to everyone.

When we say those words we are really saying, "God is our father and we are his children."

Sometimes fathers ask us to do things for them.

It might be helping with washing up.

It might be keeping our bedrooms tidy.

God, as our father, also asks us to do things for him.

He asks us to be kind.

He asks us to think about other people.

He asks us to love him.

So when we say "Our Father" we are talking to God.

We are saying, "We are your children.

We want to do what you tell us."

And now we are going to say together the whole of the Lord's Prayer.'

And that's what they did.

Mrs Jolley's children did their best to join in with all the others.

After the assembly the children went back to their classrooms.

'It's a big family!' said Joshua.

Michael bumps his head

Michael was trying very hard to be brave.

But tears kept coming.

He felt his head.

It was really quite a big bump now.

Mrs Wilson sat by him.

'I don't think you need a bandage, Michael,' she said.

Mrs Wilson was the classroom assistant.

She was very kind.

Michael tried even harder not to cry.

The tears stopped.

'How do you feel now?' asked Mrs Wilson.

'Like my head's big,' said Michael.

Mrs Wilson laughed.

'Well, it is a bit bigger than usual,' she said.

'Tell me what happened.'

'I was running down the corridor,' said Michael.

'I bumped into a big boy from another class.

He was running down the corridor too.'

'And what does Mrs Jolley say about running down the corridor?' asked Mrs Wilson.

'She says… er… we shouldn't,' said Michael.

Mrs Foster, the head teacher, came into the room.

'Well, Michael,' she said, 'I think you can go back to Mrs Jolley's class now.

It's time for whole school assembly.'

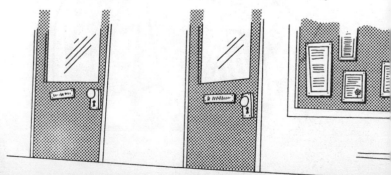

Michael joined the others as they went into the Big Hall.

David looked at Michael's head.

'I bet that hurts,' whispered David.

Everyone sat down and Mrs Foster stopped the music.

'There was an accident this morning,' said Mrs Foster.

'Two boys were running down the corridor.

One boy ran into another.

Now there are two boys with rather sore heads.'

All Mrs Jolley's class looked at Michael.

'These two boys forgot a school rule.

Which rule did they forget?' asked Mrs Foster.

Lots of hands went up.

'No running in the corridor,' said Joshua.

'Well done, Joshua,' said Mrs Foster.

'We have school rules so that we can live safely and happily together.

Without any rules we would all be bumping into each other.

But it's no good just having rules.

We have to keep them as well!

In the Our Father prayer, Jesus taught us to say, "Thy kingdom come; thy will be done."

That means that we do what God wants us to do.

That is the way to live happily.

That is God's rule for a happy life.

Rules are for keeping — not for breaking.

Then we have a happy school as well.'

Mrs Jolley's class went back to the classroom after the assembly.

Michael had a sore head for the rest of the day.

But he didn't ever run down the corridor again.

When he got home he had to tell his mother how he got the bump on his head.

I don't like cheese sandwiches any more

'Mum, can I have chocolate spread?' asked David.

'I don't like cheese any more.'

David's mother was making his sandwiches for David's school dinner.

'I'll try to get some when I go shopping later,' she said.

'But you'll have to take cheese sandwiches today.'

'Everyone else has chocolate,' shouted David.

David was cross.

David threw his school bag across the room.

David was still in a bad mood when he got to school.

He didn't join in the games before school.

He had a long face when Mrs Jolley called out all the children's names for the register.

'It's our day to go to the Big Hall for assembly,' said Mrs Jolley.

'Line up quietly, please.'

The music was playing as Mrs Jolley's class walked into the Big Hall.

Mrs Foster, the head teacher, was standing at the front.

Sitting by Mrs Foster was a lady David had never seen before.

When all the classes were in the
Big Hall, Mrs Foster spoke.

'We have a special visitor today,' she said.

'Her name is Doctor Bradfield.

Doctor Bradfield has a very important job.

She visits children in other countries.

And I've asked her to tell you about it.'

Mrs Foster sat down and Doctor Bradfield stood up.

She smiled at the children.

'Thank you, Mrs Foster,' she said.

'I want to tell you about some children who live a very long way from Daisy Hill.

They live in a very hot country.

It is a country which hasn't had any rain for many months.

Because they have had no rain, their fields are dry.

Because the fields are dry, their plants don't grow.

If plants don't grow, then there is very little to eat.

Many of the children I visit are hungry.

They only have one meal a day.

It is usually a small bowl of rice.'

David thought about his breakfast.

He thought about his cheese sandwiches for school dinner.

He thought about what he would have for tea.

Doctor Bradfield sat down and Mrs Foster stood up.

'Thank you, Doctor Bradfield,' she said.

'You have reminded us that we have been learning the Lord's Prayer,' she said.

'We've come to the words "Give us this day our daily bread."

As we say that, try to remember what Doctor Bradfield has told us.

In some countries people do not have enough to eat.

Then the prayer for daily bread becomes very special.

When we say these words, think about the children we have heard about.'

David thought hard about it.

Perhaps if all you had was a bowl of rice, then cheese sandwiches weren't so bad.

He was still thinking about it as they went back to their classroom.

David wasn't in a bad mood any longer.

He enjoyed his cheese sandwiches at lunch.

'I'm really sorry,' said Sarah

Most of the time Sarah and Rosie were best friends.

They played games together.

They worked together in the sand tray.

They shared a reading book.

They went to each other's birthday party.

But sometimes things go wrong.

It was playtime and Sarah and Rosie were in the playground.

Rosie was dressing her Barbie doll.

'That's my Barbie,' said Sarah.

'No, it isn't,' said Rosie. 'It's mine.'

'Well, where's mine, then?' shouted Sarah.

'In your bag,' said Rosie.

'No, it isn't! I looked,' shouted Sarah. 'You took it!'

Sarah tried to grab the Barbie from Rosie.

Rosie snatched it away and hugged the doll.

'It's mine,' she said. 'You can't have it.'

At that moment the whistle went.

It was the end of playtime.

Mrs Jolley asked all the children to line up.

'We're going to the Big Hall now for assembly,' said Mrs Jolley.

Rosie lined up with Hannah.

She wouldn't line up with Sarah.

Mrs Jolley's class went in from play.

They went to the Big Hall.

The music was playing.

Usually Rosie and Sarah sat next to each other in assembly.

Today Rosie sat next to Hannah.

Sarah sat next to Michael.

Sarah looked very unhappy.

'We are thinking today about the Lord's Prayer,' said Mrs Foster.

'We have come to the words "Forgive us our trespasses, as we forgive those who trespass against us."

"Trespasses" is a big word for the things we do that are wrong.

Jesus says that God will forgive us for what we do wrong if we are really sorry.

But he says that we must also forgive anyone who does a wrong thing to us.

That's not always an easy thing to do.

If someone's hurt us or taken something of ours, then it's hard to forgive them.'

Rosie looked at Sarah.

And Sarah looked at Rosie.

After the assembly Rosie took Sarah's hand.

Rosie and Sarah walked back to the classroom together.

'I'm really sorry,' said Sarah. 'She is your Barbie.

I've remembered. I didn't bring mine to school today.'

Rosie looked at Sarah again.

'Friends?' asked Rosie.

'Yes, please,' said Sarah.

'Now,' said Mrs Jolley, 'we are going to write a story.

I want you to write a story about friends.'

Sarah looked at Rosie and smiled.

'I know who my story's going to be about!' she said.

Mrs Foster finds a purse

The children were all in the Big Hall.

It was whole school assembly time.

Mrs Foster waited for all the children to sit down.

She turned off the music that had been playing.

'I'm going to tell you a true story this morning,' said Mrs Foster.

'It's the story of what happened to me yesterday on my way home after school.

I needed to do some shopping.

I needed to buy some food for home.

I drove to the supermarket.

I parked my car in the supermarket car park.

As I got out, I saw something on the ground.

It was a big black purse.

I picked it up.

It was quite heavy.

I looked inside and saw lots of money.

There were some ten-pound notes and some five-pound notes.

There were pound coins and two-pound coins.

There was enough money to pay for all the shopping I needed to do.

It would have been easy to do that.

What do you think I should have done?'

Lots of the older children put up their hands.

Then slowly Hannah put up her hand.

Mrs Foster looked at Hannah.

'What do you think, Hannah?' asked Mrs Foster.

'You should tell them in the supermarket,' said Hannah.

'They might know who it belongs to.'

'Hannah is quite right,' said Mrs Foster.

'And that's what I did.

I took it into the supermarket.

I told one of the ladies who worked there what I had found.

"That's really good news," she said.

"There's a customer here who's lost a purse."

The lady who had lost the purse was very happy.

I did my shopping and went home.

But I was thinking about what happened, before assembly this morning.

In the Our Father prayer,
we have come to the words,
"Lead us not into temptation."

"Temptation" is another big word.

It means that sometimes we think it would be nice to do a wrong thing.

I thought it would be nice to have all the money in that purse.

Then I could have used it to pay for my shopping.

But I knew it would be wrong.

It was someone else's money.

It wasn't mine.

So in the Our Father prayer we are asking God to help us to do right things and not wrong ones.'

Mrs Jolley's class went back to their classroom.

'We could play shops,' said James to Rosie.

'But you'll have to use your own play money!'

Thunder and lightning

The children in Mrs Jolley's class were sitting on the story mat.

Mrs Jolley was reading them a story.

Outside the window, it was raining.

The rain started gently

and got harder,

and harder,

and harder.

Suddenly there was a very bright light.

It was a flash of lightning.

A few moments later there was a very loud bang.

It was thunder.

There was another flash of lightning — and another loud bang.

The children cuddled closer to each other.

Sarah and Rosie held hands.

Sam started to cry.

'Come and sit by me,' said Mrs Jolley.

Sam moved next to Mrs Jolley.

'I'll let you into a secret, Sam,' said Mrs Jolley.

'I don't like thunder and lightning either!'

Soon the thunderstorm moved away.

It was time for whole school assembly.

Mrs Jolley's class walked quietly into the Big Hall and sat down.

'I wonder,' said Mrs Foster, 'if anyone can tell me where we've got to in the Our Father prayer?'

Emma thought hard.

She said the words to herself and then put up her hand.

'Well, Emma?' asked Mrs Foster.

'I think it's "Deliver us from evil,"' she said.

'Well done,' said Mrs Foster.

'Sometimes,' she said, 'we can be frightened.

It might be because we are a bit lost.

It might be because it is very dark.

It might be because we can't find Mum or Dad.

Or,' said Mrs Foster, 'it might even be like that thunderstorm we've just had.

In the Our Father prayer we ask God to "deliver us from evil".

We are asking him to keep us safe.

And God never lets us down.

If we ask him to help us he always will.

Try to remember that, next time you feel a bit frightened.

Yesterday I asked some Year Three children to write a poem about feeling safe.

Alex, in Mr Green's class, wrote this poem.

Safe is holding someone's hand,
Safe is playing in the sand.
Safe is snuggling down in bed,
Safe is having stories read.

Safe is crossing where we should,
Safe is when we're feeling good.
Safe is cuddling Mum or Dad,
Safe is sorry when we've been bad.

I think that's a very special poem.

Well done, Alex.'

All the children in the Big Hall clapped.

Alex looked rather shy.

After the assembly, Mrs Jolley's children went back to their classroom.

The sun was shining through the window.

'I think the sun makes us feel safe,' said Hannah.

And Mrs Jolley smiled.

The Hallelujah Chorus!

The children could hear the music as they walked down the corridor.

It was loud.

As they got nearer to the Big Hall it got louder.

It wasn't marching music.

It wasn't dancing music.

It was singing music.

They sat down in the front and listened.

There were lots of people singing.

There was an organ playing.

Children from the other classes came in and sat down.

Mrs Foster let the music play.

When the music stopped, nobody said a word.

At last Mrs Foster spoke.

'That wonderful music was written by a man called George Frederick Handel.

It comes from a piece of music called "Messiah".

His music is about Jesus.

Sometimes Jesus is called the Messiah.

We have just heard the Hallelujah Chorus from "Messiah".

"Hallelujah" is a word which means "praise".

Handel wrote the Chorus to give praise to God.

It tells us how great God is.

Let's listen to a little more.'

Mrs Foster played some more of the Hallelujah Chorus.

The children listened quietly.

Mrs Foster spoke again after the music.

'Today we come to the last words of the Our Father prayer.

The words are these:

"For thine is the kingdom, the power, and the glory, for ever and ever."

Those words mean just what we have been hearing.

God is very great and we praise him.

It's as if we are all joining in the Hallelujah Chorus.

But not just here at Daisy Hill School.

When we say "Our Father" we think of the whole family of God.

The family of God lives all over the world.

In all the countries of the world people are saying the Our Father prayer.

People all over the world give praise to God.

Now we are going to say the whole prayer:

> Our Father, who art in heaven,
> hallowed be thy name;
> thy kingdom come;
> thy will be done;
> on earth as it is in heaven.
> Give us this day our daily bread.
> And forgive us our trespasses,
> as we forgive those who trespass against us.
> And lead us not into temptation;
> but deliver us from evil.
> For thine is the kingdom, the power, and the glory,
> for ever and ever. Amen.

Mrs Foster played more of the music from "Messiah".

The children went out of the Big Hall.

Back in Mrs Jolley's classroom the children sat on the story mat.

'It's a big family and a big prayer,' said Joshua.

'And a very big God,' said Hannah quietly.

Bible references and prayers

The Bible reference for this book is Luke 11:1–4. By their nature the stories are short and make one point. The wording used is from the traditional version of the Lord's Prayer. The stories can be used to introduce the Lord's Prayer to individual children, a class or the whole school. They can be used as a starting point for discussion. A prayer for each story theme is given. These prayers are based on the traditional approach of a response to the leader so that the children become involved in the prayers and make them their own.

It's a big family!

Our Father,
For your special prayer,
Thank you.
For being our Father,
Thank you.
For the love you have for us,
Thank you.
For belonging to your family,
Thank you.

Michael bumps his head

Father God,
When we forget you,
We are sorry.
When we forget your rules,
We are sorry.
When we hurt other people,
We are sorry.
When we hurt you,
We are sorry.

I don't like cheese sandwiches any more

Father of all,
For those people who have no daily bread,
Please help them.
For people who have no homes,
Please help them.
For people who have no schools,
Please help them.
For people who have no friends,
Please help them.

'I'm really sorry,' said Sarah

Heavenly Father,
When we are unkind to others,
Please forgive us.
When we say nasty things,
Please forgive us.
When we want our own way,
Please forgive us.
When we are not nice to be with,
Please forgive us.

Mrs Foster finds a purse

Loving Father,
Help us to do right things,
Help us, Father.
Help us to say kind words,
Help us, Father.
Help us to be good friends,
Help us, Father.
Help us always to remember you,
Help us, Father.

Thunder and lightning

Mighty God,
When we are frightened,
Be near us.
When it is dark,
Be near us.
When we are lost,
Be near us.
When we need a friend,
Be near us.

The Hallelujah Chorus!

Our Father,
You are in heaven,
And we praise you.
You made us,
And we praise you.
You are wonderful,
And we praise you.
You are Our Father,
And we praise you.